ROGUE ASTRONAUT

Miller Williams Poetry Series
EDITED BY PATRICIA SMITH

ROGUE ASTRONAUT

MITCHELL JACOBS

THE UNIVERSITY OF ARKANSAS PRESS
FAYETTEVILLE • 2026

ISBN: 978-1-68226-286-3
eISBN: 978-1-61075-849-9

30 29 28 27 26 5 4 3 2 1

Manufactured in the United States of America

Designed by William Clift

♾ The paper used in this publication meets the minimum requirements of the American National Standard for Permanence of Paper for Printed Library Materials Z39.48-1984.

LIBRARY OF CONGRESS CATALOGING-IN-PUBLICATION DATA

Names: Jacobs, Mitchell, 1992– author
Title: Rogue astronaut / Mitchell Jacobs.
Description: Fayetteville : The University of Arkansas Press, 2026. | Series: Miller Williams poetry series
Identifiers: LCCN 2025030361 (print) | LCCN 2025030362 (ebook) | ISBN 9781682262863 paperback | ISBN 9781610758499 ebook
Subjects: LCGFT: Poetry
Classification: LCC PS3610.A356466 R64 2026 (print) | LCC PS3610.A356466 (ebook) | DDC 811/.6—dc23/eng/20250918
LC record available at https://lccn.loc.gov/2025030361
LC ebook record available at https://lccn.loc.gov/2025030362

Because the moonlight deceives
Therefore I love it.

—AMY LOWELL

From the region of his heart, a tentacle had budded. It was as long as his arm, but thin, like whipcord, and soft and flexible. As soon as he thoroughly realised the significance of these new organs, his heart began to pump. Whatever might, or might not, be their use, they proved one thing: that he was in a new world.

—DAVID LINDSAY

CONTENTS

SERIES EDITOR'S PREFACE

Remember when we whizzed right past funny?

Funny was always our refuge. No matter how implausible, numbing, and morally horrendous the news was—and lately it's been all that times at least a zillion—*something* was always worth a chuckle. Sure, we'd cringe-giggle or weep-giggle, but the giggle always won out. It kept us from officially changing our political party to "NO." It kept us from frantically burrowing a self-shaped hole to live the rest of our lives in. It kept us from throwing our smaller TV through the screen of our larger TV. A friend of mine used to say, "You know you're scraping the bottom when you find yourself in the parking lot of a 24-hour Burger King, inhaling a cheese Whopper and swilling screw-top wine."

Finding the funny has distracted us from Whoppers and wine.

You remember funny, right? That audacious fly exploring Mike Pence's head during the vice presidential debates? The first lady swatting the first man's hand away every time he zones in for an affectionate photo op. The sheer number of liars intoning "I have never lied to you."

Ha, ha. Ah, those were the days.

Then came the first signs of trouble. Comedians were having a hard time making funny. Matters which were once laughable were now—well, actually insane. Nothing said, done, or hurriedly justified was too much. Stupidity, once a detriment, became a qualification. People intent on upending our lives proceeded to do just that—spiriting away, redacting, or outlawing whole histories, destroying dissent, stunting science, exalting violence, demonizing all "others," trying to force a whole sloppy, opinionated country into a single voice.

Now they're even going after the comedians. Because funny is too close to true to be funny anymore.

Yet I come to you with the (whispered) news that poetry—be it hilarious, formal, combative, elegiac, splattered with expletives, or heartbreakingly lovely—has not yet been outlawed. In fact, we're having a ball over here.

We lack billionaires, options traders, government funding, and a huge public platform hungering for our every word and gesture. And although poets frequently pen lines and lines and lines of truth to power, power is usually occupied with headier concerns—the accumulation of more and more and more power, for instance. (And since when has being poor and powerless kept a poet from poeting?)

We've barely missed a beat. It's been interesting to watch the huddled masses discover that poetry has been veering toward true for quite some time.

How healthy is poetry in the midst of what can only be called unbridled chaos? (Ummm . . . unchecked mayhem? Rampant hubbub? Irrepressible anarchy?)

How healthy is poetry in the midst of all this mess?

Consider the three books that make up this year's crew of Miller Williams Poetry Prize finalists—Mitchell Jacobs's *Rogue Astronaut*, Raphael Jenkins's *Paper Pistol*, Stevie Edwards's *The Weather Inside*; and the overall winner, *Domestica* by Samuel Piccone.

What links these very different books is an assurance of voice, and a fearlessness that leads to moments that are sobering, relentless, revelatory—and yes, humorous. I like to think of each of these books as ideal for this particularly tumultuous snippet of the twenty-first century. They are defiant, but not mindlessly so. They are narratively and topically adventurous, sometimes playful, often new in a way that surprises. And yet they will manage to provide their readers with a needed distraction by reminding them how diversely lives and life can unreel in the clutches of a good stanza.

I'd like to take you straight into *Domestica*—and yes, I looked for an excerpt from "The Horizon Sets Its Watch," which I love, but then decided that we definitely need to hear this poem in its entirety. You'll see why.

> Somewhere, it's garbage day. The stakes are never so high
> there aren't motions to go through. Every day needs its pulp,
> another thing gone lifeless for an exterminator to usher
> into the bed of his truck. The Lord works in mysterious ways
> is another way of saying you're screwed but alive enough
> to know it. What a person swallows fills them until it doesn't,
> makes friends of the dark inside that pang until eventually
> it eats the friend. Every day's a new hell says the exterminator
> to the quiet in the cab as the world grows less mournful by the hour.
> The way an empty cage becomes an opportunity to ask,
> *do you want to keep going?* Of all the beauties worth not naming,
> it's a blessing the first name we give to anything born is blessing.
> Flowers wrecked with blight atop the weekly trash.

Flowers just because. The blue carcass of whatever was
the night before. Until something better strikes, how fine it fits.

And again:

The way an empty cage becomes an opportunity to ask,
do you want to keep going?

Samuel has obviously chosen not to toy with us. He knows we're surrounded by *all* the ugly, so we've no choice but to rout out any semblance of beauty, as dim and minuscule as it might be. As I read *Domestica* for the third or fourth time, I marveled at the poet's ability to celebrate and mourn in parallel, to face the complexities of this time and unearth lyric.

Here, from "Desert Pass":

Tell me our skin didn't draw red until the invention of the deep wound,
that stepping on a shard of ancient fulgurite only opened us, made us love
the fractal flowers of our lightning scars more. Tell me we built shelter
to un-see each other as outdoor creatures, to stay lost and fall headlong
into love's natural wreckage.

Isn't that exactly where we are? Aren't we living in the midst of "love's natural wreckage"? Among a group of memorable manuscripts, my mind kept veering back to *Domestica* introducing new ways to walk the world—not necessarily less perilous, but believing more in the power of the right words, in the right order, to lead us back toward a dim but insistent light.

Raphael Jenkins's *Paper Pistol* is also locked on to that light. It's formidable muscle in the Black struggle against our country's attempt to disappear Black people. It's work steeped in the heat of personal remembering—dissecting the potent and hurtful word *nigga*, delivering eulogies for the gone-too-soon, steeling against a mama intent on butt whupping, succumbing to the embrace of smoke, searching for a way to express the boundless joy and love that Black men are warned against expressing aloud. But in "Back to bounty," Jenkins recollects and mourns a whole gone world—

All around abounds the spoils of undeclared wars, & the nonchalance
to their undoings—in the cellphones, in the engines of cars, in the
bathwater of children, in the grayscale air. Remember bees? Remember
oceans not yet pregnant with plastic caviar? Remember when oil wasn't
a god requiring sacrifice, & there was enough for every dark corner
to be lit with a small, welcomed flame? I don't.

These poems don't confess, they confront.

As someone who has always had a terrible time coming up with titles, I was transfixed just reading through *Rogue Astronaut*'s table of contents: "None of My Friends Have Bodies Anymore," "Dialogue Between Colander and Self," "Persona Poem as Myself," "My Ex-Boyfriend Asks to Make a Silicone Replica So He Can Take Me with Him When He Moves Abroad Next Week," and the ever-popular "Jesus Watches Me Get My Ass Swabbed."

I often tell my students that a good title is a like a giant fishhook pulling the reader into a poem—but once that happens, the poem's got to be engaging enough to convince that reader to hang around.

The poems in *Rogue Astronaut* do everything but disappoint. As evidenced by his propensity for irresistible titles, Mitchell is a master of the astute perspective, the unexpected entry point, and a smart narrative flow that pulses in each poem and speaks it alive. And while you might think that the poems lean on laughs, this is thought-provoking work of quick wit and enviable depth. Inventive forms buoy the vivid lyric, and Mitchell never stops probing the new that language can do. Here's "Foreplay":

> Oh, his sweet,
> small cuss. "Shit,
> sorry I kneed you,"
> he said, pausing
>
> to check for a bruise.
> "I know you need me,"
> I grinned, having never
> been sexy, only clever,
>
> even if it meant bending
> the truth. Then he pressed
> his fist to my chest,
> kneading me.
>
> Sometimes when I am dead
> to language I remember this.

Playful? Yes. Playful? Uh . . . no.

Then there's Stevie Edwards's *The Weather Inside*, a brashly contemporary soundtrack for every single woman with the nerve to tune in and listen, and for every man who wonders why the woman in his life is so often caught gazing intently into the air that surrounds her.

Stevie writes for the broken, the confounded, and those traveling the pitted road to breakthrough. There is so much light threaded through the stanzas it's practically blinding. The wry, wistful, muscular poems confront the gnawing ache for motherhood, the insistent demands of the body, and the way alcohol makes everything better until it doesn't. They veer clear of platitudes and solace, instead daring those who intend to keep living to *let's take a good look at ourselves first, shall we?*

Here's an excerpt from "My Dear Felicity," the lean, heartrending epistolary poem to a ghost child giddily named after an American Girl doll:

> My Felicity, my intense happiness, I am sorry. I haven't made the right life to rock you to sleep. Each day I wake as late as I feel like, go to sleep when the blanket of gravity pushes my muscles into bed. Each day I cook foods I'm told children don't like (chana masala, pasta with asparagus and peas, sesame tofu). Each day I read and write poems in the quiet guest bedroom, three pit bulls swaddled around me. Each day I take a small pill to ward off your gaining breath. Some days, Felicity, I am intensely happy.

There's humor in *The Weather Inside,* but it is often an entry ramp to a harder truth. I cackled out loud at the opening to "Manifesto of a Dormant Pansexual," because I saw myself, and several thousand other women, huddling inside the lines:

> My sexuality used to be a Lisa Frank folder
> with a unicorn on it. Now it's more of a KitchenAid
>
> stand mixer, but I've got rainbows on my underpants
> for nobody to see.

Ouch. Haha. That stings. Me too, Stevie. Me too.

So. Another year, another four books breaking the mold, swaying the rafters, clearing a way through the muck. Turn off the news, log off for a while. Read what's real.

PATRICIA SMITH

ROGUE ASTRONAUT

Abduction

It hovered. In slow wind.
While he stood. Still as slate.
Clenching his bicycle's handlebars.

Its billowing feathers.
Were planes of its flesh. Encroaching.
Briefly from a different. Manner of space.

It could. See. Belief invading him.
Saw his organs laid open. Like an atlas.
Surging tributaries of adrenaline.
His heart. That citadel of sensitivity. Quickening.

Billions of neurons unskeined.
Into a single. Silver filament. Taut.

It kept. Unfurling into entireties of itself.
To teach him. With its body. True. Sight.
To pry the latent sense. Up. From his cells.

Then its convolutions swerved.
Into a sphere. Of many roundnesses.
He felt. The same shape roll. Along his interior.
Knee scrotum clavicle cheek. Like wet fire.
He spasmed. Groaned. Saw now. It had no. Size.
But was. On another scale. Vast.
Looming like its own sky. Beyond some boundary.

Holiness was simply. This hugeness. Which arrives.
As a wind from elsewhere.

To behold. To be.
Held in the. Sinews of its knowing.

It cradled. The lack of holiness in him.
Like a topaz. That it took. As he lurched.
Into the viscous light.

I

None of My Friends Have Bodies Anymore

and it's getting on my nerves. Goodbye mortality
and cellulite! Just get hooked up to a spiky hose
and sucked out as energy vapor. They act so smug

like *heads-up* and *legwork* don't make sense to them,
slang of us flesh folk. They call me *touchy.*
I tell them *keep in touch.* They're having a soirée

up at Cloud Nine or Astral Plane, one of those sky clubs
you need to be incorporeal or at least have a jetpack
to get to. From down here, the green sunset looks delicious,

reflected in a skyscraper, the windows like panels of peridot
now that the fluorescent lights are turned on less and less.
The executives have ascended like jewel beetles molting

from their too-tight armor. I'm not ashamed
to say that I love the taste of coinage, of zinc,
that archaic metal against my tongue. I wipe

a thousand-dollar coin on my arm hair
before trading it for a street vendor's lone, withered
papaya. I love my big corny tuba thigh tattoo

and stripping for my video feed, watched only
by an old man in New Estonia. You know those shirts
that apply pressure in the shape of a loved one's hug?

We all bought them back when they were expensive
and programmed them together over shots of gin and oxygen.
I'm wearing it, activating each of their embraces in turn

while another soul orgy buzzes above me
like a swarm of pastel gnats. The doctor says
the procedure would kill me instantly. My sinews

are wound fast around my delicate psychic core,
like an umbilical cord around a fetus's neck. It's congenital.
Still, I get asked to host charades. I'll mime a refrigerator,

a telescope, a janitor, an infant, concrete, the mythical seagull.
Since becoming one with everything, my buddies are entranced
by watching one thing pretend to be another thing

as our ancestors—so clever and materialistic—
used to fashion plastic toothpicks
shaped like little swords.

Soft-Bodied Animals Leave Few Traces

in the fossil record. Millennia of sea anemones
lost, their ghost lineages as branched
as their tender, unkeepable bodies.
We remember bone, tooth, shell,

chitinous exoskeleton. The hard parts.
Whatever's stiff enough to displace mud.
A spine's archipelago. I bend over
in this Utah heat, feeling the earth's vendetta

against flesh, which it punishes
and punishes then decomposes.
I unstrap my tools, trowel or brush,
to use as the rock dictates.

I had imagined grief to be the trilobite,
many-segmented and ubiquitous.
Extinction's logo. They are shrines
from the tough earth to its fierce loves

more mineral than animal.
Where is the tilde of an earthworm
that tilled the soil with its innards?
A squid's roving, nacreous eyeball?

The earth will save my hunched skeleton
but not the tapeworm that squirms inside me
of its own volition: delicate ribbon
as long and tangled as hunger. Or joy.

Ministrations for the French Horn

Cochlea, tender coil,
French horn of the inner ear.
It hears me play this rusty horn
that lately rasps.
                    I remember
the boy beside me in band class
who knew this instrument's ins
and outs. He took mine into his lap
and coaxed it apart.
                        The labyrinth
unraveled, each slide slid out
like a U transformed, new vowel
in a brass alphabet. He greased
their lengths, nimble fingertips
attuned to surfaces. The give
and resistance as he pressed
the keys. As he polished,
the flaring bell allowed his hand
to enter.
            When he placed his lips
to the cold mouthpiece, his throat
opened into its golden throat
that spoke what he spoke, but in
another tongue.
                    O, in the crescendo
of his solo, the room filled and rattled
and I realized I could love
                                a boy.
How I would dream him cradling
the curve of me, fingers along
my vertebrae, his right hand lower,
shifting, his breath
against my cheek.

Cochlea,
hidden in the motions of your hairs
lies his voice, a sound I cannot resurrect.
If only there were oil for your hollows.
If only I could coax from you
the voice that blew warm all through me,
saying, *This is how.*

Two Truths and a Lie

1. I was conceived in Minnesota.
2. Like a bad dream, my mother had me in the middle of the night.
3. My father was a muskellunge.

1. That's a kind of lumber worker.
2. Actually, it's a kind of fish.
3. He rushed into my mother teeth-first.

1. My thumbs are double-jointed.
2. One of my toes has no nail.
3. There's a rash across most of my back.

1. I was hoisted from my mother's bleeding belly.
2. These scars are where the doctor sawed off half-formed gills.
3. My foreskin floats in a jar in the attic.

1. I have a secret snaggletooth.
2. I have a birthmark on my inner thigh.
3. I feel nervous showing you.

1. For years, I slept with one leg between my mother's legs.
2. My left knee twinges if you touch it.
3. People say my skin feels cold at night.

1. I used to toss crickets into campfires.
2. I stole my grandpa's *Playboy*s.
3. I don't feel anything when people cry.

1. This dark spot on my chest is a third nipple.
2. It secretes a rusty milk.
3. I was never allowed to learn to swim.

1. Somehow, I've never broken a bone.
2. I've given people bruises.
3. You can—no, really—feel my remnant of a tail.

1. Because you asked, I have a boyfriend.
2. I love him.
3. I love him with all my heart.

1. In a moment, I will beg you to enter me.
2. In a moment, I will become impossible to touch.
3. Someone once told me I deserve this body.

Insatiable

Little brother drinks his neon sadness liquid—no one
has a healthy relationship with Mountain Dew. *Large,*
no ice. That means more pop for his buck. Who knows

if he enjoys the stuff anymore. I think it's less about
savoring those extra sips and more about putting off
the empty cup, that undrinkable last bit

that rolls around the bottom like a worm. I won't chide
him today, here in the drive-thru down the road
from Paisley Park. It's good to be fat and alive.

His arm leaves its impression in sweat on my car's
center console, and I'm disgusted and grateful.
He's bought me a McChicken for driving him.

I can't get enough of the mayonnaise with its weird
chemical spice. He sucks up the artificial citrus
and sugar with, it looks like, pleasure. Prince died

last month, an overdose, and I think of "Insatiable,"
that video where he crawls through dangling pearls.
Even if I wasn't thirsty I would drink every drop.

We drive past his studio's chain-link fence
decorated with purple miscellany: bandanas,
umbrella, panties, roller skate, ribbons that spell

WE MISS YOU PURPLE RAIN. The only purple thing
I might offer is a bottle of lube hidden under the seat.
Could be fitting. It's good to be alive and wet

and insatiable. My brother says he's glad it failed,
swallowing all Mom's pain pills. *I got the idea*
from Prince. A heap of pearls held to the lips.

The night Prince died people danced in the streets
of Minneapolis, putting muscle to their mourning,
wanting him not to be gone, wanting another song

from the purple guitar to thrum them through.
I want my brother to not stop wanting what kills us
only slowly. Grease on the tongue, fizz on the teeth.

Dialogue Between Colander and Self

Spinach-laden, dripping, I groan
through my hundred rusted mouths.
How to quell this hankering for wholeness?

    For hole-ness?

No, that is my affliction.
The enviable bowl
nuzzles its hoard of broth.

    Golden but stagnant.
    Consider hole as conduit to life:
    fishers swarm the frozen lake and drill.

Then they are ice-boring weevils.

    Just boring suburbanites
    with a taste for muskellunge.

This is not about hunger
but ache. The rims of my multitudinous holes
flinch at the chilling water
like sensitive teeth.

    So you have watched me drink?

I have watched many imbibe
and studied their flexible orifices
that clench and flare.

    We are not beyond filling them
    with food or one another's appendages
    from time to time, but in the end
    we need them empty.

And yet your wounds heal seamlessly.
Imagine the strawberry's
perpetual acne.

> Believe me, I once wanted purity of substance:
> hairless skin, un-plaqued teeth,
> a lover made of paraffin, or air.
> Air is easiest; you need only
> pretend he's there.

I cannot pretend air into iron,
to have more body than I have.

> I saw a bass with a taste
> for bass. It swallowed one
> but choked, floating to the surface
> still stuffed to the gills.

I would die (if I could die)
to be that fish.

> The eating fish
> or the eaten fish?

When one consumes
a gap is filled.
When one is consumed
the gaps dissolve.
My answer: both.

> Then I will toss you toward the sun to dry.
> Taste the oxygen, rusting one.
> Know that you are being eaten
> by the sky.

Dumb Dead Dad

And me here eating off-brand raisin bran
and liking it. It is my favorite.

I am not good at being angry,
not when a steel spoon

offers me my globular, upside-down face.
Its rim scratches my tongue's easy itch.

I admit, Earth could have been a little bigger.
Its mountains not so sharp. More fruits.

They want to build a colony on Mars.
They will suffocate in burnt sienna.

They want to build a colony among the clouds of Venus.
They will suffocate in atomic tangerine.

Forests burn each day and still I am so
stupid happy. I take naps and I sneeze into the sun.

I am sorry for mortgages and vodka.
I am sorry you wanted things with rigors

like love and children
and the intricate talismans kept by men.

Tell me now, as you rinse off in some emerald brook:
what habitat could have nourished you?

What planet can you finally call *home*?

Rogue Astronaut

Space is not exotic up close. Beyond my helmet glass,
lunar craters etch no face. The scarred topography of Mars
reveals no marvelous canals. Just the cold drama
of matter colliding with itself unawares. Bright, dumb comets.
At first I'd yearned to cavort through a primordial carnival,
enrobed in nebulas dyed pink and gold.
At first I'd readied bone and muscle for survival
and return, for cradling again a man more elegant
than mathematics, for kneeling to conifers before they all unravel
into ash. Eight little planets suckling the Sun's heat?
No. They're rock, ice, gas.
Blur my vision and even Earth dissolves into void.
Human culture was like eating: a rich, unsightly dream.
I can't recall if I cut my tether on purpose, an urge
to trade everything for dark. I've honed myself into
one vector, drifting windless beyond galaxies,
connected to the never-to-be-known by the material of vacuum.
There is nothing between me and the most distant pulse.
If other life exists, I arrive alone, loosed from language,
gender, the memory of touch.
Headed for that absolute expanse where neither day,
nor night, nor twilight can unmake me.

Unicorn Contortionist

Here's the moral: a unicorn was not enough.
We craved her mythic body exotically twisted:
back curled backward on itself, muzzle peeking
between her hind legs, horn grazing her pudenda.

Audiences drove home itching, dreamt of new,
effervescent appendages entering them.

Her trainers sharpened her horn with diamond sandpaper,
polished it, applied gold leaf to its spiral groove.
They tied tinsel into her tail. To coax her to bend,
they brushed her hind hooves with peppermint.

Alone in her stable, bent too far, she pierced her colon,
and panicking, jerked and ripped a kidney.

They found her splayed, mouth open, beside a brown-red arc
splattered by her dripping horn's last wild motion.
She was buried in her plexiglass box in the compact pose
that culminated each show. They snapped her stiffening joints

to fit her in. Hunched, embryonic, she evolves into bone,
her illustrious spine white as sugar, which she loved.

Hypnos

photograph by Wilhelm von Gloeden, circa 1900

Wide-eyed, oracular, the boy stares through the photographer's lens
a century into the future into the eyes of a boy his age, me, as I clutch
the heavy book in a library basement. Delicately, he holds to his chest

two pale flowers—*Brugmansia*, or angel's trumpets—whose bitter petals
can dilate the pupil, induce trance. My thumb traces them. The leaves tied
in his downy hair. His cheek, his lips. My calves, asleep, stick to the tile floor

as the prickle travels upward. Envy for the boys on the pages, eagerly naked
or absentmindedly naked, or in togas slipping off the shoulder. Nothing
to unbutton; fabric with the will to come undone. I didn't care then

for the art of it, ancient Greece reanimated, only for the bare fact
of the models' softly veined forearms and penises, each foreskin an
unopened calyx. These boys, plucked from the sands of Sicily, just becoming

conscious of their loveliness. Last week, Huy wove me a crown from willow
and asked me to model for his new camera, there in my underwear
at a beach from my childhood. But the beauty he insisted I held

in my jaw's angle, the curve of my ass, was spoiled by my failure to strike
the pose. Hips to the side, torso straight on. *Relax. Breathe. Don't squint.*
No smile. When my crown unraveled and fell into the water, he stopped.

I sympathized. I wanted to keep the image of Huy wading to his knees,
also in his underwear, lens cap tucked into the waistband. His body took
a form I couldn't frame, didn't try, while my form was one he couldn't keep

even as he framed it. That night, Huy's tongue against my crumpled
circumcision scar. Envy become wistfulness, not for the Sicilian boys
who are long dead, but for my own loveliness wasted in self-effacement,

my boyhood smothered in hand-me-down polo shirts. Hypnos's eyes
held the silhouette of the man who made him a young god, Gloeden
backed by bright sky, or maybe those were fluorescents behind my head

as I hunched over the glossy book. In the next photo, the boy was smiling,
mortal, the two flowers gone. Within the hour he would wipe from his cheeks
the homemade blend of glycerin, milk, and olive oil used to mask

his sunburns. He would step back into dusty trousers to await the moment
he could see his picture. In my photograph, the one Huy never sent me,
I stare a century into the future into the eyes of a man my age,

who will have ripened into shapeliness as some boys always do,
even in squalor, or especially in squalor. He is alive. My body is awkward
and gone. When he thumbs the straining muscle in my back, he trembles.

Persona Poem as Myself

The face that I inhabit protrudes
into contemporary air.
The mole below my lip is punctuation
to anything I whisper,
expressing a fond perplexity.
My body is young, impossibly young, arranged neatly
in cells of muscle and skin, pert skeleton.
I contain my future. I tug it gradually
from my throat like a heavy chain.
My intellect and my personality huddle close
like twin eggs, brimming with innuendo.
Famously too vain to wear my glasses,
I easily mistake a large cloud
for the torso of my current lover,
maybe even his nipples if I squint.
He fills the sky only to be dissipated
with theatrical poignancy by the wind.
My homosexuality, an iridescent plasma
running lazily through my circulatory system,
attunes me to loss and to beauty,
including and especially my own
as I gaze out upon untraversable marshes
that I have wished ever since childhood
to jump naked into. Not today. Not ever.
I stand proud with my average posture,
wearing my accidental clothing,
then kneel into the loam of bland history
that accepts such singular and ordinary knees.
When I close my eyes, I forget I am not invisible.
My elbows twitch.
Gone, for now, the interruptive wit

that leaves a film around the shape of myself
in rooms of people, their ears pulling at
the shape, the film in ecstasy lifting
away from my stubble, my voice gymnastic,
my heart a sharp, silver anchor.

Men

1. Men Running

Nowadays a man seldom chases a deer
until the deer collapses from exhaustion.
Often a man runs for no reason at all.
Even the most contoured of thighs
jiggle, gelatinous in motion.
Oxygen, sharp and hot,
shoots through each leg's
fractal of arteries.
Just over the horizon something quivers,
waiting to be cut open.

2. Men Standing

Their paunches push staunchly outward.
Their backs curve shyly inward.
Sometimes they forget they are creatures of nuance.
Inside their torsos, organs hang
like soft chandeliers.

3. Men Squatting

He is playing checkers, naked.
Bent at the knee, bent at the waist,
he folds in thirds like a rejection letter
written on crisp, heavy stationery.
His invisible intellect perches
atop the long worm of his musculature.
The tip of his genitals
traces in the sand a numeral
to be used in secret arithmetic.

4. Men Sitting

A man has dreams of a bare room
filled with circular porcelain stools.
His gluteal fat squishes against the flat seat
into a Rorschach blot.
Were someone able to look down at it
—even the man himself—he would say
it looks like a sort of butterfly.
But the shape is hidden by what makes it.

5. Men Lying Down

They would like to be hollow
as a chocolate rabbit
and, for that matter, made of chocolate
that melts from its own warmth
into the weave of the fleece blankets.
But their pelvises are protuberant.
Their spinal columns,
like overcooked shish kebabs, sizzle.
Some lie straight.
Some curl on their sides.
Some splay their limbs toward sleep
in erratic configurations,
as if their physiques might form the single key
to an ancient, now misshapen lock.

The Cuttlefish

i.

Whatever the cuttlefish know,
their tentacles cradle private.

A school of them approached,
withdrew,   approached,

studying the eddies stirred by our kicking,
our arms and legs an oddity to them,

smooth as nudibranchs but stiff,
and our snorkels the fluorescent antennae

of some garish crustacean.
Or maybe their inscrutable eyes—

pupil shaped like a W—discerned
exactly what we were:

the patterns of our body hair,
where it spirals, parts, or converges,

even the direction of light waves
bouncing off our swimsuits' nylon.

ii.

A proper Floridian, you scan the beach
for glass: brown rarer than clear,
green rarer than brown . . . an et cetera
you rattle off for me by heart.

I have not studied the ocean's whims
and hierarchies as you have;
nor, I suppose, has the ocean
in its egalitarian churn.

Your five-toed waterproof shoes
tread over minor shells, over windrows
of kelp whose leaves are air-bubbled,
you explain, to keep them vertical

in strong currents. Vestige
of a botanical intelligence deeper
than sentience. I, for one, dare not
stomp the branched fan of coral

or the sand-flecked, sun-bleached rubber
of an abandoned swim mask.
Litter or artifact? Depends
how long the sea had kneaded it.

You fling a green shard toward the water—
edges too sharp, needs more time—
for someone as attentive as you
or for a future you to find.

I wish I had a lantern of red glass.
to shatter into the tide
to be churned to garnets over decades
in a lobster's gastric mill.

iii.

You lift something: white, flat, oblong,
longer than your hand. You turn it over and back

to guess which way was up, the body
a ghost around its bone. Watching the ribbons

of waves from below, could this cuttlefish
have imagined our twin ocean of air?

Beneath deep sky, your mind configures.
Wind brushes moisture from the bone.

EXOSPHEREHPSOXE

is scrawled red with stick pen into his sketchbook
deep   as if carved through to the artery
visible from the back   when I turn the page

EXOSPHEREHPSOXE

raised scar   that I trace with a fingertip   and yes blood has shrieked
across our linoleum   the carpet corner   we don't
discuss   Mom's ruined finger   eternal bruise ring
this love she trades her body for   her son   made of moon
who maps the heavens in red   concentric circles
the world's unwieldy symmetry   made into relic

EXOSPHEREHPSOXE

is the outermost layer   where particles of air do not
touch   where an angel   could cup his palms around
a molecule of nitrogen   it's that sparse   that far
gone   that abstracted from
our warmest moment   of having shared one body
on the computer screen   me   controlling Tony Hawk's direction
him   maneuvering the tricks   on the other end of the keyboard
pulling off a kickflip   heelflip   grinding the length
of a helicopter blade   which somehow made the wall burst   into snowfall
and we grabbed with our pixelated hand   the secret cassette
glowing gold above the half-pipe   as if an angel's mixtape
had dropped down through the thermosphere   then the plasmasphere's
garish aurora   crackling ionosphere   vast mesosphere

is a shield that wards off sleep   because sleep is   when the devil spies
is   when the devil whispers monosyllables
slit   fork   groin   squelch
sunrise   is the messiah chanting   palindromic nothings
at the top of his lungs   until Mom screams
stop   stop   stop   stop
echosphere   stratosphere whose churning radiation seeps
into everything we drink   look   there is an inaccessible planet
inside of the Earth   is there my brother   inside of
this brother   chugging Monster on the porch daily   out of him pours
an acid waterfall   over the edge   along the side of the house
frozen come winter   a pale yellow
that starving opossums come to suckle
and the wicked   will feed   on your nectar
and the frail   will be anointed   with ash
shut up or I'll put my cigarette out in your eye   he prays
to our mother

ƎXOSꟼHƎЯƎHꟼSOXƎ

melts experience into mirage   an old envelope   of photos
he says are fake   fourth-grade soccer portrait   he tears up
that's not the real me   the real him haunts   his sketchbook
a ghost in graphite rubbed out   redrawn   rubbed out
redrawn until his teenage self has 10-pack abs
and bulging traps   he is stuck there for hours   in the armchair's
soiled carnation print   we really did garden together as kids
out behind the shed   in summer heat   snapdragons marigolds dianthus
black-eyed   susans and bleeding hearts   they really were
called that   it happened   it happened

pulling a good memory like pulling a weed by the root
chromosphere   radiosphere   troposphere
with its government cameras   whose mirrors allow them to blend
into bare blue sky

makes him dig out the GPS tracker   implanted in his fractured knee
wade   through a sea of stale laundry crying
where are the tapes   *tell me*   *the tapes the secret tapes the tapes*
behind the wall   so now a garage-sale portrait   of George Washington
hangs in a wrong spot   over a wrong hole the size
of his wrong cranium   a garrulous minotaur moonwalking
through his nervous system   the bad
magenta electricity   *I have to find I have to find the*
helicopter can't you hear the helicopter
always something hidden   just beyond the jittery surface
something beautiful   turned upside-down   his eyes
so blank   intense   their green-brown watercolor
like the watercolors   he stopped painting   one day

echoes when he puts on the holy purple mantle   with its Vikings logo
zips it up   his Godhoodie   now he must must must
when he veered and crashed during a hailstorm
the pellets   pockmarking the Honda   were divine confetti
pummeling so fast so loud the car reverberated with a voice
beneath the frequency   of human sound   it said
this is your trial   *yours alone*   *but you will live to share your goodness*
the sun emerging turning the sky of ice into gold aslant
and he said   *I will I will I will*   and the sky
turned to liquid   and the car   was totaled

represents *the confluence of the celestial layer with the alchemical boundary*
condensating ozonether in the hyper-latitudinal altitudes' quasarozephyrs

so sayeth my brother
whose friends evaporated like rosewater
that is purified into perfume to enshroud each encephaloid entity as exemplified
in the ~~psychosphere~~ ingeniousphere a dense tiny circle
his head I think at the center of it all
red cosmic nucleus
he stares up into a distance away and away
will I meet you again someday
in the exosphere

We Play Donkey Kong

Jungle patterns unfurl across our eyelids like fronds of dream; we take turns dying; we love to watch each other die; when the death tune plays we flex our fingers, ready; I thumb the joystick; you thumb the joystick; muscle memory tautens, drumming the buttons; we revel in instinct, in adrenaline, in this the apotheosis of tool use; we watch each other inhabit apes with increasing fluency; their polygons contort elastically in acrobatic leaps; they eat gold bananas; we eat plain bananas, suck pixels of sugar from each other's lips; they grunt, shriek, hoot; we clap each other on the shoulder; they shoot from cannons, slap bongos with absolute consistency, wallop lizards into non-existence; they dance; armadillos tumble off the edge of the universe; inside the code, a 1 becomes a 0; you squeeze my wrist; dappled light from outside plays atop the screen unnoticed; birdshadow darts diagonal across the room; a car alarm blares silently; we transcend skill, transcend mastery; our textures intersect; furs interfoliate; with unthinkable precision we phase through boulders, traverse the hollowness on the other side of existence; sun falls; night's border hurries across landscape; we do not, cannot sleep; with wrinkled palms, apes palpate the boundaries of their physics, shivering inside the hardware; inside our bodies we clamor and gnash; on a tree in Madagascar an indri sings a territorial warning; fire rages; bulldozers encroach; the indri sings a mating call; swing jazz plays on loop; digital bass, indefatigable saxophone; a glut of bananas; your ripe stench; the taste of indri flesh, a morsel of extinction; they howl; amid neon foliage we howl; all night your pupil's a green globe and I live there, begging for eternity.

Nice Bike!

People tell me I have a nice bike.

They say, "I bet you have a lot of gears." Or, "I'd like to see your drivetrain."

Once I let a woman examine my drivetrain. She crouched down and ran her finger along various metallic components. "Yeah," she said. Her hair was red, like a lobster.

There is something about my bike that is excellent. I don't know what it is. But I have the bike.

It's silver. That's cool. But also, normal?

Its tubes—or beams?—are sturdy. Sturdy enough that it functions properly as a bicycle.

The kickstand is totally right there when I need it.

Maybe I don't deserve this bike. Maybe it should be wrenched apart and distributed among those who appreciate it. When they tell me my bike is nice, what I hear is, "You have a surprising dearth of knowledge about velocipedes."

Velocipede is an old word for bicycle. That's about it.

I realize now I may have implied that lobsters have red hair. I meant that the lady's hair was the same red as a lobster's carapace is red. I thought that was obvious, but it is possible I have a special knowledge about a lobster and its components.

People ask, "How much did you pay for that bike?"

I used to say, "I don't know. It was a gift." This answer is true, but unsatisfactory.

Sometimes I say, "$3000," and they say, "Whoa!"

Sometimes I say, "$50," and they say, "Whoa!"

I assume the real price is somewhere in the middle.

Every day, I worry about somebody stealing my bike. I had to buy a very expensive lock. I can't tell if that's ironic.

I used to leave my bike standing loose outside the old diner, until a guy in muddy jeans tried to mount it. The sight of his sweaty fingers around the handlebars was revolting. I pounded on the window from inside and he ran away.

I tried to spray-paint my bike to ward off thieves. Pastel yellow with white stripes and red polka dots. Kind of a deviled egg thing going on. Now people say, "Wow, you have a nice bike. And terrible taste."

I love my nice bike. Not because it is nice. I think if I understood the way it is nice, I would only be able to love the niceness, and the bike itself would be hidden there inside of the niceness, feeling neglected.

I like my bike because when I ride it down a big hill, my stomach floats and I don't think about anything.

I like it because, from the side, it is shaped like a katydid. See it? The part with the seat is the antennae. The front tube is its long hind leg.

No?

Foreplay

Oh, his sweet,
small cuss. "Shit,
sorry I kneed you,"
he said, pausing

to check for a bruise.
"I know you need me,"
I grinned, having never
been sexy, only clever,

even if it meant bending
the truth. Then he pressed
his fist to my chest,
kneading me.

Sometimes when I am dead
to language I remember this.

Tonight I Am Any Body and No Body at All

Is there other life?
  I stare out my shower's window, through Orion's
  polygonal window   into deeper void.
And do they have something like ass hair
that they hate on themselves   and scrape away?
  My milky way of blood and cream
  swirls down the drain.   I lie down
human and smooth   for just myself
and this psychedelic gummy cube
  and the vibrator's futuristic curve: rocket
  me away. Think—   they might not feel pleasure
or the chemical mirage that pleasure is,
or shame   or thirst. But is that conscious life?   Self-
  conscious life?   I need to know
  I'm not alone   in needing to know I'm not alone.
The Hubble Deep Field's   bacterial swarm of galaxies
promises that life repeats a billion-fold
  at every scale.   And isn't it cruel not to feel
  for their betrayals and firework histories
and arsenic-based emotions   just because
they're far away and might not exist?
  When I get high like this   I have so much empathy
  it stretches hot toward eternity   and runs out
of things to enter. Is there   other life?
Only in this state can I 100%   believe there is.
  There's the thing   from *The Thing*, hopping star to star,
  no form of its own, only what it borrows,
sneaking into evolutions   to wear their jewels:
skin and wing and shell   and breath.   Then moving on.
  Ultimate space queer, all costume,
  stripping off everything   but knowledge.

Some humans, I think, could humble themselves
to that invader.   To kneel,   be absorbed.
   To try on another body as it tries
   on yours.   I've seen the need in people's eyes,
that tiny wet gloss in the dark.   I've shown
that need. It never quite   comes real.   We come
   apart, still whole. The oily membrane around the self
   heals shut.   Once someone gripped a tangle
of my chest hair, said   *I could get lost in this*
and I was distracted from trying to get lost in the shape
   of him,   compact,   requiring less
   from this melting world.   Pressing him to me,
I felt I was small, smaller   than anything,
and also   I was huge,   huger than him, as huge
   as a world.   Trying to escape the planet
   of myself,   I invaded a lot of different people
for a time,   and part of them
didn't survive it.   Their hearts burst out
   and scuttled away from me on crabs' legs.
   Their skulls opened   into fleshy flowers
and tried to swallow my face   in vengeance
and part of me didn't   survive it.
   Some substance twirls around some star
   that is not flesh   or nerve   or brain   or throat
but is what it is   and lives to live
and I am on the verge   of the verge
   of crumbling   into understanding it.
   Tonight, how I adore all my former lovers.
I want to kiss   their foreheads while they sleep
and pull their blankets up   a little bit
   as if it is my place to do that.
   My grand tour of affection before . . .
before   what? Before I go   hazy and bright
and float into the sky to become a constellation
   and sometimes   at just the right slant of October
   I am visible above the tree-ragged horizon

and they look out from their porches
and think,   "We all loved him,   didn't we?"
    Tonight, I am any   body and no   body at all,
    exploding into an infinity
of crab nebulas   that scuttle
into every nook   of every heaven
    we might never reach.

Mercury Vapor

i.

After weed s'mores, stamping out the fire,
last sigh of the coals—
            Forgot these were Dad's old boots. A little loose.

And this camp lantern he could dissect
and reassemble (too bright,
turn it off).

Hadn't remembered him in months,
but this happenstance of burn and chill,
like his flicker-face in firelight—

            Easier to picture Icehouse beer,
which in the cold garage he guzzled alone.
Tongue grazing the sharp aluminum aperture.

"You know, I think he started drinking because
he was afraid of becoming a father," Mom once told me.
            I chomped a carrot darkly.

Campsite ghostly pale. Addicted ants
on metal skewers jawing up marshmallow scum.
Midnight, but I can see everything.

Blood drains from my cheeks in monochrome.
From where the light? Is he watching over? Could—
                        Oh duh, the moon.

Blinding disc. Abrupt.
Watching. "Wait, did he ever tell you

about the UFO?"

ii.

I want to believe
it haunted him.

Hovered over the dead field,   rotating black
against the blackening sky.   Hard-edged   and shuddering.
Its wide ▭ made of light
swimming in his teenage eyes.
Twinkle in your father's—

Which would mean it wasn't me that scared him nightly to the garage
by being not exactly there, not quite
how a kid should—

"Thought they'd implanted a tracking device,
might return and find him."

The distance between him and it   unknowable,
no referent   in the blank sky, or in
his mind's sky,   darkening.
And the ▭.

His need to claim light
so that light would not claim him again.

Four hours, vanished, when he became a null him.

To fit entire office buildings with his bright globes,
make them bulwarks against the dusk.

Driving into crystal Minneapolis,
me in the passenger seat, lost in sleep.
Rhythmic mercury vapor streetlights across my eyelids.

Not the light that can take a boy and undo him
if he begins to look upward,   dreaming colors
in the crushed velvet sky.

iii.

TV flashes from six years old:
fangs brown ooze eyes
rolling back into the skull.

"But Dad, it says it's rated R."
Alien: Resurrection *Predator* *Fire in the Sky*

Flickering ▭ in the dark living room.

Silver curative ribbon of film.
Reliving his deleted scene.

A poster in the *X-Files* says I WANT TO BELIEVE.
Its tin disc floats, dinky and menacing.

I want to believe beyond body. Not to be touched
by those beings, but touched with their entire
being. Deep reverberation
caused by a sense organ we do not have.

Because what could he have felt that he did not have words
to tell even himself?

And what he heard: a speaking
with what were not tongues
making what was not speech.

iv.

With burly fingers, he plies his trade of glass. Cradling
the incandescent bulbs. Balancing atop a ladder
to lower a fluorescent tube
into my hand.
A fragile baton.
"Careful, careful." Smiling,
explaining wattages and lumens:
measures of energy and brightness. I,
the son. High pressure
sodium lamps along the road. His arm around my shoulder.
"Those were my design." I
pull away. His wrist hairs, pinched
between his watch's silver vertebrae.
I rub my charm bracelet, a birthday gift from Mom.
"She making you wear that?" Pewter heart and butterfly.
Bringing me to a store's display of lemons. Then
the store across the way, whose lemons appear to gleam
from within. "Which lemons look better?"
Metal halide bulb shines with an electric arc.
"These," I say. He lights this grocery chain, I know.
Growling "your Mom's a wacko bitch" in the garage.
Fluorescent crash.
"Women will fuck up your life."
Warning me not to touch the shattered tube,
but the vapor's in my lungs, the phosphor coating
like moth wing dust already on my fingers.

v.

"I'm Marvin. Like Marvin the Martian."

Yell-whisper in my ear over the electro-
thud of club music. Strobing face sipping

a green drink. In this palpitating now spaceship.
I say my name and he doesn't hear

and I say it again and he doesn't hear
and I smile and am no-

body, smiling. Turns me around,
rubs his probe against my butt so I will want it

for real, will have been waiting years
for it, will take it, will not be able

to take not having it, metallic pang
just too deep as my eyes glaze over

seeing the future of not being able to recall
this man, just a name, did it even

happen, the color and the lights,
and the hands and the hurt and the good,

nothing true in this shit mud drunk brain.

vi.

A museum room the color of memory, dim.

A hospital's room of bilirubin lights
for those born yellow with jaundice.

A bright, flat ▭ on the wall.
No instructions, no sound.
Only the *no* of the ▭.

He approached the transparent chamber
where his child, blindfolded, bathed in light,
baptized into blue.

I step nearer. Its surface unchanging.
Something in it that is wrong.

Bulbous head, sick skin, hands so—
a creature not of this world.

A step out of time's corridor.

I reach. My hand sickens, entering
the ▭ that is not flat
at all, that is made of space.

Through the portal, touched
the infinitesimal hand and it was decided.

Weightless churn.
Gravity's dead sparkle.

Yellow heap of him on the bed.

"Do you want us to remove the breathing tube?"
The *yes* of my mouth.

Floating in the impossible span.

vii.

He'd led me to gather birch bark
for tinder. Fire, a miracle
I had no curiosity for.

I was distracted: flannel fibers
draped on a sumac branch, torn from his shirt.
Wrapping them around and around

"Hey, stay close to me."

my finger to watch the tip go red, purple,
exact burgundy of the sumac berries,

complete concordance of self and
plant, camouflage, dye,
blood, stain of

Earth saying

"Stay close. Stay—

Apse with Stained Glass Triptych of the Crucifixion

Inside a space one minute large, I kneel, looking into the window

of my phone screen. Video call from my brother, hoisting himself onto the railing of our mother's fourth-floor balcony. His beard glimmers. He has poured a bucket of rainwater over himself. His words reach out toward the glass between us. They are urgent; something he wants me to do; I cannot comprehend. My words reach out. And does he hear.

Tell your brother he is not the messiah he claims. Tell Jesus he is no king, commands no nation, rides no caparisoned horse.

He will say earthly things are only shadows cast by the true things up in heaven.

He will say the people here are empty. The real ones are in paradise.

How an act of violence evolves: it should not have happened; it could only have happened this way; it was preordained to happen; it was, in a grand sense, good that it happened.

The passion, in the moment, was untidy. Wet hair clinging. Asymmetry of blood and bruise. Pressed over centuries into thin glass between two forces: belief and impulse toward beauty.

A man cannot temper himself into a god, even if his dying is extraordinary. Someone else must build the elegant windows.

Tell your brother you have not betrayed him, did not call the police that are coming through the door, coming to drag him inside, drag him to the ground.

Tell your brother not to jump. Tell him not to hoist himself upon a cross that no one else can see.

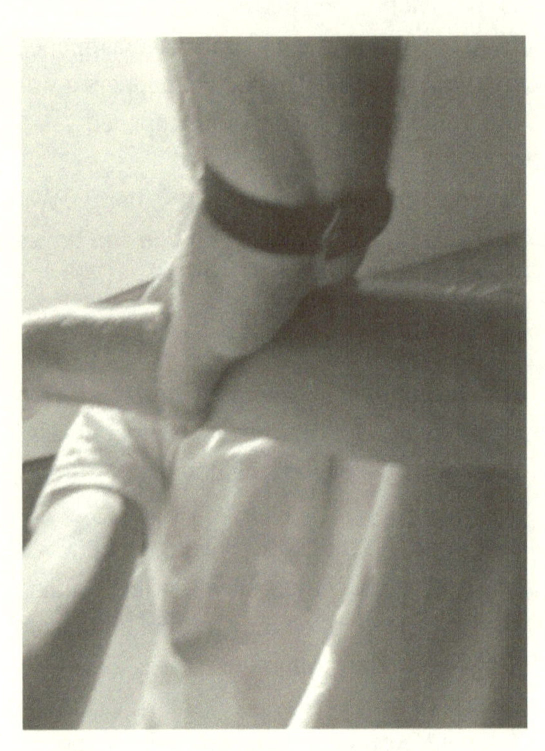

Faith is a thing that other people have: flexible, utile, a digit that does not fit in the glove.

Before he ran to the balcony with her phone, he had wrestled her to the floor. For half an hour, he pinned her arms, yanked her breasts for leverage, anything he could hold on to. He believed he was the one fighting for his life. This flesh beast in the guise of mother, her untested strength.

He is one to whom miracles are always happening. *Thank God somebody found him. Thank God he didn't get his hands on a knife. Thank God she called 911 in time . . .*

Who can save themselves from the savior's perfect logic. *I am eternity. To deny is to deny yourself eternity.*

Who, kneeling while light through colored glass illuminates their face, can tell him *no.*

I have been told that when the call dropped, it was because they forced his wrists behind his back and knelt on him.

Angle of arms. Angle of sky. Rictus of a feeling I do not know. No beauty there. I cannot put it there.

When Mary wept, the crystal of her tears did not beautify the corpse. It was too soon. Jesus was a person.

He should not have been made to suffer; he knew he would suffer; he was willing to suffer; he suffered for the future.

You can touch the glass, but not what looks at you from in the glass.

There is no tense in which he did not suffer.

IV

Venice Pier

. . . , . ; . . : , : . ,

thinks a moon jelly,
sensate halo

shed by whom for what trespass?

Maybe one of these studious far-apart midnight fishermen
who had a flesh thought
like I am thinking always
about you; I was never good.

Diatoms collide . . . . . with the jelly's tentacles,
pinprick noticings,
and contractions ferry them to its tolerant hole.
Food in, waste out, sperm, eggs.

Entities impress upon it only correspondences:

passing jacksmelt , a shape of altered dark
frond of kelp ;;;;; gentle pressure severally all over.

It pulses downward at your cell phone's flash—
put that away, come near.

Flesh *is* thought, say my fingertips ' ' ' '
on your neck, my thumb poised '
against the pulse that thrums above your jawbone.

Biomass is an idea about itself spreading.
It wants more surface area, nerve-stitched.

O

under moon tonight do you not feel

observed?

By minds who stroll a boardwalk above

while we are here suspended in our matrix,

eating words like necessary meat.

Love, let us be true   for our voyeurs,

invite their flash—

Tongue against tongue, our senses map each other

: : : : : : : : : : : : : : : : : : : :

Still Life

Over your tulip tattoo,

        a thin sheen of our cum,

near-clear as the glaze on

        that vase you molded at

the pottery wheel, wet

        clay flower blooming

outward and then inward

        around its gentle emptiness

to be christened with glaze

        as the act of making

becomes the made thing,

        hardened into permanence

by brute, exact flame

        to hold one rare tulip.

At the Immersive Van Gogh Multimedia Projection Exhibit

The beginning is perhaps more difficult than anything else,
but keep heart, it will turn out all right.

In gold script, any sentence by itself on a purple wall
is about life. But was it "all right"?
As if he didn't famously . . .

Google tells me Vincent was writing his younger brother Theo
who'd started a new job. Words of quick comfort. That's all.

In the vast room, irises
tongue open across all surfaces
to rhythmic synth, quivering on the cheek of a woman
taking a selfie against the wall,

And look, Theo died six months after him, stricken with grief
and also late-stage syphilis. *All right, all right . . .*

on children splayed out like starfish, the floor blue
and blooming but never quite
that moment of blue stillness, and then the garden melts
into brushstroke crows
computer-edited to flap.

I reopen yesterday's email to my younger brother:
It took real persistence to extend your flow to this length.

Which was not about life
but about his latest rap lyrics,
sent to me as grainy jpegs: pages inked edge to edge
with interwoven rhymes
that I could map, yes, grazing each pointillistic syllable
but unable to hear the lush

composite indigo wringing the night sky radiant—
    would I have been that fool
who used a painting to fix a chicken coop, but now
    it's worth 50 million dollars?
Of course not. We would have plucked *Sunflowers*
    from his sensitive hand,
given him the cash, a hug, maybe it would save him.
    We'll buy a mug from the gift shop.
A yoga mat. Pour one out with old Vincent.
    Lie down with old Vincent.
GOTTA GOGH? reads the sign for the restroom.
    And I remember that joke:
Kill myself? Killing myself is the last thing I'd ever do.

        Google tells me Homer Simpson said that.

    The bandaged self-portrait
materializes while horseflies buzz, before it fades
    into the faces of townspeople
he met, some of whom disliked him. Something of too much
    care, or fear, in their features
rippling and twisting—that by stepping into the work
    we step into his brain?—
into triumphant abstract fanfare of technicolor paint.

        This song's my masterpiece, my brother typed.
        Each line's worth one million dollars.

His fingers wrenched the patio table apart, punched
    through a window, and also
adorn this handwriting with swirls and loops and serifs
    as the words go on.
More beauty. *More* pressure. *More*—   Somehow
    only now I see
the severed ear was not an act of art.
    A squirming sun sets
over peasants and yellow wheat, while Édith Piaf
    who drank herself to death

sings, "Non, je ne regrette rien." I'll admit,
    it's beautiful to bask
in this house of his mind, but I could not have
    shared a house with him.

It's just, and don't get angry when I say this, I'm not sure
what these lyrics mean. What is it you're trying to tell people?

My brother refreshes his SoundCloud, waiting
    for a single download.
When he offers me his roll of pages, like a bouquet
    plucked from winter,
I look for a gold coin to place in his rough hand.

Mutant

Coaxing a fruit fly larva from its vial with a sterile brush, I think
of that self-portrait
in which you hover between masc and femme,
of the paintbrush stroking you as it rendered you: ashen face
unsmiling on an ashen backdrop, gaze tilting away,
in your hair red petals like a hot
aortic bloom.

—And I jolt from my task, recalling pain,
how this pale bundle is wild
with nerves and still-moving mouthparts
and suffers soundless in colorless blood as I
extract its heart,
examine its vitals on a microscope slide.

Your palette knife dipped into the crimson.
You applied a nauseous stroke to the canvas.
Your works are filled with neutrals, grays or browns,
the shades of burned things, or those
yet to burn.
This flower is a rare vulnerability,
a tender, exposed, fiery activity.

Like your cigarette's tip amid smoke.

I realize I have swollen with affection
for the maggots I pull apart from either end
with forceps. The innards empty in unison from the tube of skin,
a cluster of imaginal discs,
the proto-organs,
transparent and intricate
with possibility.

One disc has been altered to express
a green fluorescent protein,

                                        a glow seen only in the dark.

I have watched bodies, awry and miraculous, grow suspensefully
into maturity. The *bithorax* mutant fly
has a double-segmented chest
                                                            that flares into a double pair of able wings.
                                    My art takes shape
in golden flies with spiral wings,
flies that walk forever backward,
        starry night flies' swirling hairs.

        Beyond love for any one of them,
I tighten the ribbons of their genome
while my dish of ethanol, the fly morgue,
fills.
      You rinsed your brush. The water clouded red.

When you showed me, I did not recognize the pallid face
as you. I assumed the wound
                                                        was an accessory.
        I could have reached
and brushed your shoulder then.

Were you beside me in the darkroom,
I would offer you my microscope's view:

an insect, its interior,
        its kindled, hidden hue.

When I nudge the focus, it blurs
                                                            as if watercolor:
you are tying a flower made of ribbon, green,
into your charcoal hair.

Mirror

That morning,
I helped him install
the last of many mirrors,
the one above his bed,
with mounting tape.
His eyes narrowed within it.
He didn't know
anyone besides me in the city yet.
He said he's glad we met organically,
the first guy like that in a long, long time.
It's rare.
I agreed,
feeling special.
He has a lot of know-how for someone
four years younger than me.
He roasted squash with oil and anise
and I became attached
to his little hand-waves, grinning kisses.
An idea of home.
Each day that week, more furniture
from IKEA, frantic screwing
atop a vast rug
beneath his string lights.
We played Nintendo—
bought by his old sugar daddy,
he admitted, before recounting orgies,
circuit parties, outdoor fun.
I laughed, relieved that I could share
my own history, although
my breath got weak when I pictured him
with other people.
In his glass gallery
there are spots where I am doubled

This evening,
he posts on Instagram
his apartment of mirrors
and in the caption,
invites followers
to private message for a visit.
I didn't know
you could advertise yourself like that.
In turn, these guys will enjoy, needlessly,
his slow seduction: food, music, card game,
the dare,
a greedy
feel, and all
the rest. Does he understand the risk?
Four years ago, I learned
not to cook dinner for guys, or else
they'll become attached.
What for me had been a simple kindness,
they took for more.
Each guy is most exciting at the first:
one half himself, one half
a vast expanse
of whisper, hidden light
that fades by day—
the process gets old. Or I did.
I had hoped to embody an entire orgy
atop, inside, beneath, around
him. Failing that, to make him into
the orgies I never had.
So why do I get hard when I picture him
with other people?
On my glass screen
his nearly naked pose is tripled

or quadrupled | then sextupled
or an infinite row | then an infinite scroll
of men in orange underwear, | of different-colored jockstraps,
embers reaching into the distance, | zoomed in or out by my finger,
but only one of them is | like the finger of a god,
warm to the touch.

Mustache

She has fallen in love with Groucho Marx. Specifically, with his character Mr. Hammer in *The Cocoanuts*. Or rather, with the actor playing Mr. Hammer in the stage production downtown. Three times she's watched him cavort amid the plywood tropics, throwing himself about with nimble buffoonery, zesting the air with puns.

At home, she mimes gags in the mirror, her limbs waving like palm leaves in a sudden warm gust. When her roommate walks in, she explains, "I'm doing Zumba."

She sips cocoa from a mug with a mustache printed on the rim, watching the snow pile up. The lawn flamingos, buried, blushing through.

Furtively, she purchases a hammer.

How she yearns to be the checkered vest and pinstripe pants that hug his spindly frame. Dare she imagine static charge between his bushy eyebrows? His sharp-witted tongue pressed softly to her throat? With Sharpie, she draws a nose and spectacles above her pubic hair, teasing into herself a plastic cigar.

The last show, she brings her bright orange purse and finds a vacant seat up front. The scene comes where he scurries down into the audience to steal something, and then it is happening, he is grabbing the purse from her lap. Inside he finds only a pair of Groucho glasses. She has outwitted him. He stares at them, puts them on, and everyone laughs.

When he looks back at her, she is wearing a pair of her own. The distance between them has vanished. It is like she is kissing him from inside his own face.

My Ex-Boyfriend Asks to Make a Silicone Replica So He Can Take Me with Him When He Moves Abroad Next Week

I have to stay hard
as the mold hardens
so he leans over the tub
and I kiss him harder.

As the mold hardens,
I feel it clench
and I kiss him harder.
I squeeze his ass, press against his hole.

I feel it clench.
Now reluctant to let go,
I squeeze his ass, press against his hole,
but time is up.

Now reluctant to let go,
the mold holds my form,
but time is up.
We marvel at the detail of its negative space.

The mold holds my form
in my absence.
We marvel at the detail of its negative space.
He could even thrust into this

in my absence.
It's smooth, has enough give.
He could even thrust into this
to savor the contour of our difference:

it's smooth, has enough give.
I could pour the gel into his hollow
to savor the contour of our difference,
fill myself with his silicone inverse.

I could pour the gel into his hollow
or use this one we worked so hard to make,
fill it with my silicone double.
He could take the real me tonight

or use this one we worked so hard to make,
his souvenir.
He could take the real me tonight
while I clench around the shape of

his souvenir.
I could kiss him goodbye, hard,
while I clench around the shape of
what I bury in him.

Close Encounter

Forgive me, loveliest. I cannot conceive
of your eleven ears at once.

I lick the one
shaped most like my own,
making my ear its analogue,
my lobe in sympathy tingling, splitting,
as I paint my tongue across
the complicated frills:
texture of root and taste of bronze.

One by one I touch, become
pliant sieve, taut coil, ruffled sail,
and so on to eleventh heaven.

To think, the people of Earth
regarded each naked other
as alien, fumbled their not dissimilar genitals,
fumbled the planet into ruin.

Briefly, I endure your wet appendage
venturing into my nostril.
But I do not pretend delight
in that particular opening.
To pretend is failure.

I direct your crystalline eye
lower, guide your facile broom
as you signal me to take into my hands
that spongy fruit within a fruit
at your very core.

We simmer and bloom,
I dare assume, in unison.

We are like one creature.
We are like a creature that will not evolve
for yet another trillion years.

Alien Lullaby

pronounce this, child: is for the aperture beside your heart
is for the sensitive filaments
knotted near others but when alone
in the distance, see the towering of dry ice
beautiful how gleams when it covers the hill
we enter sleep through an iridescent upward
touch your upper teeth, your teeth, your lower teeth,
taste the spread oily on the rock between us
speech whistles through the jutting into our throats
but I cannot quite say ; I have always lacked something
no in my eye
gravity tugs my all the way through
when one moon rises, the wriggle from the ground
when the second moon rises, they so loud, so sweet
we were made for this but it fights back
beware the that hunts with its skin
I lack a though you will surely grow one
I hope your will not twist inward like mine
when you were born, an eon of ended
you emerged platinum and slick with
tangled in , the fabric woven from live nerves
I gave up all my and it was worth it
hear the sulfurous thundering
hear the blow between the throbbing cliffs
still not enough symbols for the I need to teach you
in case you are spangled and like me
count the smooth on each of your heads
now with your , hold this thing with no word
and be on the red horizon
beckoning, , even after I am gone

My Own Private New Hampshire

I rented a room 53 miles west of Venus
so I could be with my college boyfriend
who dumped me immediately. He lived
next door, in another dimension. To get him
to notice me, I took aimless walks
in electric blue pants, like some sad
horny alien. I would have done anything
except call him. The B-52's sang to me
from my hail-pocked Honda's tape deck
about runaway poodles, a bottomless pool,
and when to kiss the pineapple between
a lover's legs. Which is to say, after kissing
his stomach. Which is to say, never again.
My walls were strung with purple constellations,
Christmas lights for mood lighting. In case.
This was the techno-future, 2014,
except I couldn't afford a smartphone
so everyone's invisible conversations
ripped through me like gamma radiation.
Instead of raves, I ran around graveyards,
imagining the dead in love triangles,
love rhombuses, perverted love parabolas.
My dad had died that spring, but he didn't
belong to the dead and their interstellar
daisy chain. He was in that middle space,
a foggy soundstage barren as the moon,
knotting and unknotting his paisley necktie
on loop. It's where Ricky taps his foot,
rocks his hips and guitar neck back and forth
in the video of "Give Me Back My Man"
that glared from my laptop screen. Ricky hadn't
died of AIDS yet. That would be in five years,

so 29 years ago. Barefoot, Cindy
turns around to look at him, her brother,
on a riser above her, wearing shades.
I'll give you fish. I'll give you candy.
I'll give you everything I have in my hand.
What my clenched hand could offer
was a sweaty clump of Swedish Fish
from the planet's longest candy counter:
waxy, melted together, red dye #40
seeping outward along my palm lines.
I didn't want to go to bed with a stranger
and tie a bow of caution tape around my neck
but I did. My shirt with squids on it
absorbed my stupid tears, squirts of ink,
while I sat on my car's dented hood
and leaned against the windshield's firework-
display of bug guts. I took off my clothes
and touched myself beneath a satellite's
slow strobe. On treeless summits,
it turned out I could stack a cairn in memory
of anything, and somebody would balance
their own lopsided rock on top. The air
was so sparse. When I finally drove back
to Earth, I sprinkled glitter on the highway,
only the glitter was that shiny crud
that gathers in your eyes from sleep.

Jesus Watches Me Get My Ass Swabbed

How many sexual partners have you had
in the past year? the patient intake form asks.

Lifting my head to do some mental math,
I see a portrait of the Virgin Mary on the wall.

If she were sitting here, pressing the clipboard
not too hard against her ripe conundrum belly,

she'd pencil in a zero. I lowball my number.
May we pray with you today? I check *NO.*

Mary would pray, her unzipped hoodie billowing
as she follows the nurse down the hallway,

wondering, "How will she judge me?"
Which is what I wonder, feeling the tightness

of my nice underwear I wore for some reason.
I am brought here by no divine summons,

though each boy had the voice of an angel
at the time. In the white exam room

there's a cross on the wall with dead Jesus
or dying Jesus—I've never been sure which.

The white tissue draped over the big chair
seems almost sacred. Then, reverse communion

as the nurse takes my blood, scrapes some cells
from my throat. She explains that gonorrhea

can infect via the anus, and tentatively asks,
"Is that something that might apply to you?"

So I have to shuffle down my skinny jeans
and face the wall, where Jesus cocks his head

with curiosity, watching the sins he died for.
The insertion of the rough Q-tip is unlike

a nail, though it still feels like punishment.
Maybe it resembles the sting of holy conception,

which Mary recalls, tensing her spread thighs
while the nurse prods and says, "Are you telling me

no sexual partners?" Mary puts a palm on her stomach
and flinches at her son's torture on the wall, thinking

how her goodness was pierced with goodness
to let him in, and she accepted, and he

is to be pierced with cruelty. "You understand,"
says the nurse, "that your body is a temple."

I nod. Mary nods and takes the pamphlets
about food stamps and when the heartbeat starts.

The temple of Jesus's body is ravaged
by wood and nails. He opens his mouth

as if to say, "I have never felt so alive."
As if to say, "I forgive you."

Selfie in Tyvek™ Windbreaker

after James Merrill

My newest retro-punk accessory
Tumbles from an envelope that's made
Of Tyvek, too—what cheerful symmetry—
Into my hand. One-day delivery's
No lie. Thanks, Prime! Across its night-black sleeves
Constellations pop in orange and teal. Taurus,
My sign. Right on the sternum, white Polaris,
Epicenter of the Day-Glo galaxy.

It smells like something died in it: the Nineties,
Maybe? Turns out, the fabric of the cosmos
Is wrinkled, thin, and vaguely unctuous.
The universe—not so vast—fits just right,
Though the elastic rides a little high.
I smile, consult my phone with its smashed glass
That doubles as an electronic mirror,
Finger-brush my hair, and snap a selfie

For the free-for-all panopticon
Of Instagram. Everyone's *everyone's*
Ubiquitous voyeur. Random men,
In gregarious spirits, rumble my phone
Like a digital Ouija to compliment
And proffer pixelated hearts. Séance
Via screen, vis-à-vis the living dead-
Eyed. A social medium, I respond.

"I found it thrifting!" Plausible, but false.
"Isn't it . . . *far-out*? You know, because it's space."
The nebulae applaud my wit, all traced
In phosphorescent ink. Off to the closet,
Shorts down, for a glow-in-the-dark thirst trap.
Self-satisfied, I grab my AirPods, cap,

And fabric mask, then shimmy out the door,
Grooving to a techno satellite waltz.

On a bike, a girl with neon pizza socks.
A mustached guy jogs past, pocket-watch
In his skinny jeans. Must be tight on time—
No, wait—just walking his chihuahua mutt.
In no rush, I pause to antique window shop
The typewriters a hundred bucks a pop,
Seeking the keys to simpler thinking, for
Computers, sleek, only worsen writer's block.

Anachronism is the latest look
For us not-so-youths. Nostalgia's all the rage.
Just peer into this store called Bettie Page:
Pink walls and posters of bikinied babes
Hotter than full-on porn. A faux Wurlitzer
Enhaloes a rack of pleather corsets.
I'd try one on if I could stomach it.
Or at least I'll claim I did on Facebook,

Which makes me weirdly old. I choose which face
To punctuate the post: the crying laugh,
The wink with stuck-out tongue, the round-mouth gasp,
A monkey with its hands over its eyes.
See no evil. Read between the lies.
Middle schoolers browse on Apple tablets
For online Edens with their flavored truths
And my memories of MySpace have no place.

I browse *The Ideal Book* from 1900,
Hand-bound by T. J. Cobden-Sanderson.
(My Kindle has a crooked PDF.)
Retired, he crouched atop a bridge by night,
"Bequeathing" to the Thames his loads of type.
The metal punches plunged into the river's sand,
A rippling ode to integrity of craft.
Inspired to write, I leave his book unread.

Each new quip greets the public as a Tweet,
Hypertext haiku for the suburban sage.
Imagine the time it took old T. J. to lug
280 characters. That's ten
Whole alphabets, plus period and comma.
His tone would be too heavy for the genre,
Anyway. These days it's sass and wrath.
The self's a brand name. Id and id compete.

Hence, presidential upset Donald Trump,
Blowhard Messiah of the blond and sunburnt
Whose red-white-baseball-capped esprit de corps
Is rather grim. Obama, their bête noire.
At rallies, they shoot up with sparkling hate,
Electric drug I, too, have come to use,
Now tapping at my phone for breaking news,
Impatient to be mad, to gape, struck dumb.

Although, when I could be struck down by bullets,
American technology fresh-made
By AMMO Inc. smack-dab in Hollywood
For me, the everyman, I think I should
Allow myself a jagged inward scream
Now and again, instead of seeking out
That rush felt by a guy whose gun makes me
More fragile than the sleeve from which he pulls it.

Along my forearm's a vector of red,
The night sky's longitude, pointing to Cancer.
Ominous, but my fate's no certain bet.
My torso's a zodiacal roulette.
Will I go down as Virgo, the virgin?
Doubt it. Water bearer Aquarius?
If I indulge that hereditary urge
To drink myself onto my deathbed.

Or Scorpio's slow venom? If my blood
Festers with that virus. Two tests ran clean,
The third reactive, bubbling in some flask.
The Norns are torn. BETTER NOT TELL YOU NOW
A Magic 8 Ball taunts. DON'T EVEN ASK.
Perhaps I'm taking this apocalypse
Too personally. My leaky faucet drips
And I hunker down to chronicle the Flood.

Yet, when the day of reckoning rolls in
And the dead rise in tailored suits, or the nude,
Or gym wear, depending on the rules,
I might request a chat over calamity
With you, Jim. I feel I have the right,
My initials being yours in inverse,
Your white windbreaker the yang to this
Ectoplasmic yawning-abyss yin.

For now, divination by syllables.
This poem, clone mostly, grossly measured out
In 18 stanzas of 8 lines (blankish verse,
Book-ended rhymes) so that your spirit hand
That summoned mentor spirits of its own
Might stir by déjà vu and enter mine,
Elastic-cuffed. My screen-addled brain has no
Vocabulary for this parable.

My spine's grown hunched from shouldering the World
Wide Web, one of a race of Atlases.
All us high-tech vagabonds groom our beards,
Hoist data bindles across the cyberscape.
Google this: a cartoon evolution chart
Plotting the arc from knuckle-loping ape
To *Homo erectus* (cue middle-school jeers)
To Man at Desktop's embryonic curl.

Too blatant, us holing up in apartment wombs,
USB cords our umbilical lifeline?
I'd buy it. Our generation's kitsch relics
Will not last to be vintage—obsolete
Before the update's due. Our river of garbage
Flames at the entrance to the underworld.
Lacking T. J.'s mettle, I have no letters
That will survive their tossing into the fumes.

Take this handful of plastic Scrabble tiles—
EARTH melts, is rearranged as HEART, its tear
Of R dribbling down to crown AGE as RAGE
Plus a slippery V to mark the GRAVE.
HE BOUGHT A LOT FOR LIST OF HONORS SEE RECEIPT
FEEBLE SIGH IF THE LAST HERO TOO SOON CORRUPT
FACE OF PILLS ROBOT EROS TEETHES ON OUR THIGH
—My shifting epitaph upon the burning piles.

I Clean Dead Bed Bugs from Inside My PlayStation

without gloves or pity. A surprise civilization that fell,
maybe, when I left town to hike the Appalachian Trail,

thinking I was strong enough to finish. They, too, resorted
to comfort, huddling beneath the warm battery, mating
atop the memory drive. This one rode the carousel

of the interior fan while I pummeled the controller,
shooting arrows into an alabaster jaguar with one wide

and vulnerable eye. An unprecedented experience
for the bed bug and for me: one more real than the other.
When the polished claw pinned me flat, I thought, *Shame*

that I was born into a universe where I cannot perish like this.
Sweat on my high-definition cleavage, adrenaline pumping

my unrendered heart. The discarded exoskeleton
balanced atop my cotton swab is as weightless as
an angel on the head of a pin. Not that I can elevate

a bed bug into beauty, beatitude. Its husk too ugly
for my brain to love, this amber-glass cast of its soul

if it had one. And after a moment of blankness
I was reborn on a grassy ridge with a pouch full
of healing herbs, my failure erased. *God, to be sexy*

and sexless under a bustier of embroidered hide. Not
shriveling in front of an enormous screen, too lazy

even to quell my nightly hunger. Squandering my
powerful thighs, tools of the hunt. I almost admire
these determined insects, bodies built for pure utility.

Their strewn legs scrawl a history on the plastic slab.
A puff of canned air, and they rearrange. Gone now

on the face of an alcohol wipe. For many nights
I harvested the viscera of feathered wolves, wiped the soil
from my photorealistic face, and chewed. I'd never noticed those

who ruined themselves in the black box. Who craved
my heavy blood with their entire hollowness.

Chronicle with a Series of Vessels

Mushrooms sprouted from my temple
and ate their way through me
until nothing was left. I used them
to make a soup. I slurped myself up
with elaborate spoons. Obviously
this is a lie. I was merely the oak
who watched it all happen.

They cut me down. I was heavy
and had such an appealing grain.
I was made into a cabin so quaint
that I moved in. No furniture,
no bed. Oh well. I hung myself
a wooden frame that held a photo
of myself. The man in the photo

is mid-blink. I think I was afraid
to press the shutter at the right time.
All roads from there led back there.
I removed my biological clock
and put it under the floorboards.
My carrots grew. Grizzlies eyed me
hungrily, and I was flattered.

When I died they cremated me
and poured me into a prehistoric urn,
the type of thing I might have crafted
had I been around. The cabin burned.
The picture of me inside burned.
I mixed the ashes into my ashes.
It was all very convenient.

I keep the urn in the credenza
beside the porcelain soup tureen. Now
a giant owl pellet, I arrange my face
of regurgitated hair and bone. A shame
I never managed to meet myself
as myself. Every mirror I see is broken.
No, not cracked. Just plain broken.

Ultraviolet Catastrophe

With all possible tenderness, I shine a laser—
    red to green to violet—into your pupil,
        whose tessellated mirrors and sensors shift:
a calibration we cannot perform on ourselves.

    Like a child at the dentist, you squeeze my free hand,
        ceramic on skin, sensation that confuses
which is whose. Metal eyes feel no pain,
    none of our new parts do, but there is still

        sensory intensity, the old reflexes.
I stop. Your hazel irises cloud back in.
    Perched on the edge of the bed,
        you leave an indentation in the quilt,

its pattern of atlas moths diving inward
    toward your gravity. So many fabrics
        we have worn out over the decades
on one bed or another, while we persist,

    replacing each organ as it withers.
        I do not mourn the diminishing territory
of flesh, your remaining patch of cheek
    I stroke, then the titanium cheek that is,

        I would say, equally yours, equally original.
Information, tyrannical and absolute,
    falls like hail from the stars, radiates
        from every particle always. Science, spongy

and half-made as an early limb,
        has evolved into articulated shapes
                to catch it, mold it. I touch the bionic stent
at your neck that continues an artery

        as a polymer tube, its mesh intricate
                as several forms of art. You exhale,
take up the laser, shine it in my eye—
        red to green to violet—my entire vision

                violet. Centuries ago, the ultraviolet catastrophe:
our equations said a heated object would emit
        unseen light of infinite energy. We had measured, also,
                that this was not true. But the world cannot err,

only us. We watched our theories rot away
        like a hand or part of a face—we had wanted
                such things to stay, they had served us
since before memory—but then

        the quantum suture. We grafted a new physics
                atop the wound, flexed it, cool and supple.
What part of me remains when the whole of me is dead?
        you ask, smoothing a patchwork moth. I say, *We have*

                shaped science, and science us. I tell you I am ready
for the synthetic brain, the heart. The materials
        we have inhabited fall away behind us, beautiful husks,
                laying bare—ever new, ever tender—this love.

The Ultramundane

Pluto. Pluot.
Flecked, forgotten orbs.

Dense with juice, the pluot meditates
at the fringes of the produce section.

I palm its weight, hungry
for new flavor, hungry

to prostrate myself on a desert of nitrogen ice.
To be anywhere but back in town for a month,

helping my brother learn how to exist.
"The Finns have a saying:

own land strawberry, other land blueberry."
Fidgeting open a plastic bag,

he gives me a dry chuckle. Decades of practice
and I still never know what to say.

"It means there's no place like home,
but you know, some people prefer blueberries!"

Oma maa mansikka,
muu maa mustikka.

Home's all bleed and sugar.
Alien land's a tartness that has its time, its pull.

Turn of the century, Percival Lowell yearned to find Planet X,
that invisible source of gravity.

His sister Amy smoked cigars, kept a pistol
in her desk, penned yearning lesbian odes:

you are remote from me as a bright pointed planet . . .
Her affection stretching out for light-years.

My brother gets anxious when we reach the self-checkout.
"Can *you* do it?" he asks. "I can," I say brightly, "but you can, too."

He looks at me with wide quivery eyes
like I'm holding some comical awful

life-saving syringe. He can't find *Pluot*
on the spinny plastic tube with all the produce codes,

starts batting at it until it spins and spins
like the impossible rolly plastic log barrel at playgrounds

where you can try to run on it but after a few seconds
you'll always slip off.

Neither of these plastic cylinders has a name that I know of.
I can't find them on the internet, which makes them hyper-precious,

like jewels that would oxidize if exposed to light.
Unnamed, undiscovered, the glint of Pluto

was caught on film at Percival's observatory
but he thought it was just a star.

When the stroke took him suddenly, no one told Amy
because she was stuck delirious in bed. Gastritis, neuralgia.

I call out for you against the jutted stars
And shout into the ridges of the wind.

Lines written not for him. Were they close?
Is sharing an obsession one way to love?

I know who will call me if my brother dies:
my aunt. Mom wouldn't be able to handle it.

Could be he jumps naked from a window again.
Could be he has a panic attack, sprawled

on the hood of a parked car, and the police
slam his face into the sidewalk and snow and rock salt

again. And I jet off to California, writing poems
about things he can see that no one else can see,

his brain's spinning kaleidoscope overlay
on everything, even the walls of his room.

Percival squinted into his gargantuan rotating telescope
to view the face of Venus in broad daylight.

Hour by hour, he sketched a shifting network of spokes
like a dark, injured spider stretching its legs

across the hemisphere. He'd narrowed the aperture too much,
his telescope turned ophthalmoscope, casting onto Venus

shadows of the blood vessels in his eye.
My brother eyes the Taco Bell sign,

beacon in the bare blue sky.
"Want me to win you a burrito?"

He goes right up to the impossible coin game
of slippery underwater platforms

housed in a plastic hexagonal prism that also has no name.
Swear to God, he can land a free burrito every time.

Some trick of the nickel's angle into the aperture, an intuition
of fluid physics, the velocity of metal quivering as it sinks.

They hand him his cheesy, beany, paper-wrapped prize
and he hands it to me, and I don't deserve it.

Is it enough to write this? To have tried at care?
Amy loved feverishly, wrote methodically,

and when she died critics wondered
if, really, she'd been capable of love or poetry at all.

Damn the critics. They killed Pluto
and some Taco Bell executive had the coin games taken out.

So yes, this was all a while ago. I've been telling it a little weird
to give this proof,

that certain kinds of knowing
exist outside of time.

My brother's still the best at something.
Planet X is out there.

ACKNOWLEDGMENTS

Many thanks to the following journals, where some of the poems originally appeared:

American Poetry Review – "My Own Private New Hampshire"
Black Warrior Review – "Two Truths and a Lie"
Cincinnati Review – "Tonight I Am Any Body and No Body at All" (as "The Thing")
Gulf Coast – "Mutant"
Iowa Review – "Apse with Stained Glass Triptych of the Crucifixion," "EXOSPHEREHPSOXE," "Dumb Dead Dad," and "Foreplay"
Massachusetts Review – "Ministrations for the French Horn" and "Men"
Missouri Review – "Unicorn Contortionist"
Ninth Letter – "None of My Friends Have Bodies Anymore"
Passages North – "Chronicle with a Series of Vessels"
Pleiades – "At the Immersive Van Gogh Multimedia Projection Exhibit"
Ploughshares – "Insatiable"
Poetry Northwest – "Soft-Bodied Animals Leave Few Traces"
Quarterly West – "Jesus Watches Me Get My Ass Swabbed"
Revel – "Hypnos"
Water-Stone Review – "Dialogue Between Colander and Self"

"Apse with Stained Glass Triptych of the Crucifixion" was awarded the 2024 Iowa Review Prize in Poetry.

"At the Immersive Van Gogh Multimedia Projection Exhibit" was awarded the 2024 Prufer Poetry Prize from *Pleiades*.

"Chronicle with a Series of Vessels" was also included in *Best New Poets 2019*.

"Soft-Bodied Animals Leave Few Traces" was featured on *The Slowdown* podcast with Tracy K. Smith.

Thank you to Patricia Smith for selecting this book and to everyone involved in the Miller Williams Poetry Series for making it a reality.

I am lucky to have had a number of truly generous mentors. Thank you to Cleopatra Mathis for showing me what poems can do and for encouraging me to write an honors thesis in poetry. Thank you to Donald Platt, Marianne Boruch,

Bob Hicok, Dana Roeser, and Adrian Matejka for helping me find and hone my voice as I put together my master's thesis, especially the day Don and I spent hours rearranging my poems at a conference table. Thank you to David St. John, Robin Coste Lewis, Anna Journey, and Susan McCabe for prompting many of these poems during workshops, and to Mark Irwin for pushing me to imagine a wider scope for the book and for guiding it through its final stages.

I am so grateful to Charlie Peck, Ashley Dailey, Anthony Sutton, Megan Denton, and D. A. Powell for being close and honest readers when I have needed extra thoughts on a poem or manuscript draft. I am grateful as well to my fellow writers at USC for such insightful and formative workshop discussions: Amelia Ada, Akhim Alexis, Taneum Bambrick, Mayookh Barua, Bryan Byrdlong, James Ciano, Marcus Clayton, Darren Donate, Alisha Dukelow, Matthew Gelman, Alexandria Hall, Ricardo Jaramillo, Liz Johnson, Erin Lynch, Krishna Narayanamurti, Michelle Orsi, Kathleen Maris Paltrineri, Eve Payne, Catherine Pond, Crystal Powell, Tom Renjilian, Austen Leah Rose, Lindsey Skillen, Sophia Stid, Leah Tieger, and Jorrell Watkins.

Thank you to the Fine Arts Work Center and the Frost Place for support for my writing.

Thanks to David Haydon for being the arm of the law in one of the photos in "Apse" and to Lucie Noon for being the mother.

Thank you to my friends Marissa Allen, Katie Chung, Allegra Condiotte, and Errol Culbert for being supporters of my work, and to Colleen Cowdery for inspiring much of "The Cuttlefish."

Thank you to my seventh-grade English teacher, Kathleen Patrick, for showing me early on that it's okay for poems to be "touchy-feely," and what it means to be a poet.

Thank you, always, to my family. And eternal gratitude to my mom for encouraging my early interest in poetry and reading me countless books when I was a child. I miss you.

NOTES

Epigraphs: From the poem "Moon Haze" by Amy Lowell and the novel *A Voyage to Arcturus* by David Lindsay.

"Insatiable": The quoted lyrics are from the song of the same name on the album *Diamonds and Pearls* (1991) by Prince and the New Power Generation.

"Unicorn Contortionist" was written in response to a prompt developed by Audrey Gradzewicz.

"EXOSPHEREHPSOXE" references the video game *Tony Hawk's Pro Skater 2*.

"Tonight I Am Any Body and No Body at All" is inspired by the 1982 horror film *The Thing*, directed by John Carpenter.

"Mercury Vapor": The museum room in the sixth section is inspired by *Iltar* (1976), one of the Space Division Constructions by light installation artist James Turrell.

"Apse with Stained Glass Triptych of the Crucifixion": All photos are courtesy of the author.

"At the Immersive Van Gogh Multimedia Projection Exhibit": The quoted letter was sent by Vincent to his younger brother Theo in January 1873. Vincent was nineteen years old at the time. The exhibit is *Immersive Van Gogh* by Massimiliano Siccardi, though liberties have been taken with the order in which images and sounds appear. The Homer Simpson quote is from the third episode of *The Simpsons*, "Homer's Odyssey."

"My Own Private New Hampshire": A number of images are inspired by the B-52's album *Wild Planet* (1980), especially the songs "Private Idaho," "Strobe Light," and "53 Miles West of Venus." The quoted lyrics are from "Give Me Back My Man." The phrase "glitter on the highway" is from "Love Shack" on a later album, *Cosmic Thing* (1989), made after guitarist Ricky Wilson had passed away from AIDS. Chutters, a store in Littleton, New Hampshire, really does have the world's longest candy counter.

"Selfie in Tyvek™ Windbreaker" is a pastiche of "Self-Portrait in Tyvek™ Windbreaker" by James Merrill.

"The Ultramundane": The quoted lines are from "Wheat-in-the-Ear" and "The Taxi" by Amy Lowell.

www.ingramcontent.com/pod-product-compliance
Lightning Source LLC
LaVergne TN
LVHW051011080826
845145LV00009B/2564
* 9 7 8 1 6 8 2 2 6 2 8 6 3 *